ISBN 978 0 720005134
Text: Elin ap Hywel
Editing, Design and production: Arwel Hughes, Mari Gordon

Also available in Welsh

Inside front cover: PENRHYN SLATE QUARRY by Henry Hawkins (1822-80)
Penrhyn Castle, The Douglas Pennant Collection (Accepted in lieu of tax
by HM Treasury and allocated to The National Trust in 1951).
©NTPL/John Hammond

national slate museum
amgueddfa lechi cymru

# Contents

Welcome to Gilfach Ddu, home of the National Slate Museum. These buildings once housed the workshops for the former Dinorwig Quarry. Built in 1870, these workshops are on a pattern similar to a British Empire Fort. The central courtyard, clock tower and marvellously detailed windows give them their unique character, still visible today.

These workshops catered for all the repair and maintenance work demanded by a quarry which, at its height, employed over 3,000 men. The quarry galleries high above Gilfach Ddu echoed to the sound of the great explosions that freed the slate from the rock. Below, the workshops would ring with the music of hammer and anvil, mallet and chisel. Between them they supported an industry which exported thousands of tons of slates from Wales to the four corners of the world.

Dinorwig Quarry closed in 1969. Today, rather than fashioning wagons and forging rails, the workshops tell a very special story: the story of the Welsh slate industry. Here you can travel into the past of an industry and a way of life which have chiselled themselves into the very being of this country.

You'll hear a gripping story, from industrial unrest to the small details of everyday life. Strikes and suffering, craftsmanship and community: all the drama of real people's lives.

Gilfach Ddu was the heart of Dinorwig. We needed a pretty big heart for the whole quarry, as 3,700 men worked there when I went to the quarry. So we needed a pretty big heart to supply it with everything.

**Walk with us into the quarryman's world . . .**

# USING THIS GUIDEBOOK

This book will guide you around the workshops and rooms of the National Slate Museum as it is today – from the Engineer's House at one end of the site to the Fron Haul row of houses at the other. Every so often we will pause on our journey to find out more about the background of the slate industry, from 'how was the slate extracted?' to 'what kind of life did women have in the slate quarrying communities?'.

A handy map in the centre shows the different parts of the site and the location of all amenities.

# WHAT IS SLATE?

Slate is essentially mud that has first been compressed and compacted, and then squeezed and heated by the Earth's forces. Dinorwig Quarry slates originated as mud deposited in the sea during the Cambrian era of the Lower Paleozoic Age. Movement of tectonic plates formed the mountains of Wales, and provided the pressure to change this mud into slate. The high quality of the slate is a result of the purity of the original mud, and sufficient pressure and heat.

Sericite mica, quartz and chlorite are main components of slate, along with small amounts of hamatite and rutile. Tiny variations in the proportion of some of these minerals can lead to a rainbow of variations in the colours of the slates themselves – from different shades of green through grey and blue to a deep, rich red. Nine layers of slate run through Elidir mountain and they are called: green and wrinkled, redwood, old quarry blue, new quarry blue grey, new quarry blue grey mottled, sage green, willow green, bronze and purple red.

# WHAT CAN YOU MAKE FROM SLATE?

Welsh slates may well be the best in the world: they are easy to split yet very strong. These qualities mean that they are particularly suitable for roofs (water and ice don't affect them at all), billiard tables and laboratory tables, and electrical switchboards (slate doesn't burn or conduct electricity). In Tudor times, slates from the Penrhyn Quarry at nearby Bethesda were used to roof the newly restored cathedral at St Asaph near Rhyl. Hundreds of years later, the slates are still there despite the worst ravages of the weather.

Slates are also used to make all kinds of beautiful decorative objects – sundials, candlesticks, bookends and a host of other items. You can buy gifts such as these to take home with you from the Museum shop.

But what about the rock not used to make the best slates? In the past, quarrying a ton of slate could yield as much as twenty tons of waste. But today everything is used: as bricks and tiles for houses, to build roads, and – in the form of very fine powder – in toiletries such as make-up and talcum powder. The slate industry may be closer to you than you think!

# QUARRYING SLATE

Dinorwig Quarry was carved out of the mountain itself – Elidir mountain, high above Gilfach Ddu. The first step in the process of quarrying slate was to free a piece of rock – which might weigh hundreds of tons – from the face. The quarrymen would drill into the rock and fill it with *powdwr du* ('black powder') or explosive. One man would place a fuse in the powder and fire it before running to join his workmates in the blast shelter.

The blasting happened at particular times of day.

After returning to the rock face the men would need to clear the rubble and any precarious sections of rock. Two

quarrymen would then turn the slate blocks into 'pillars' of 100kg-200kg each with a cold chisel and a hammer. Another two members of the team would be working in one of the open sheds. Having pillared the blocks into rectangular slabs, one of the men would then split them into different thicknesses, depending on the quality of the rock. Using a wide-bladed splitting chisel and a mallet of African oak he would aim to get 16 slates from the one piece, depending on the quality.

Rules for Blasting

1. Blasting is allowed hourly, at the end of every
2. SIGNALS:
   A RED FLAG will be hoisted upon a spicuous spot for Seven Minutes during blasting operations
   Also a STEAM WHISTLE will be blo thus :—
   ONE WHISTLE means that the men mu retire to a place of safety: after the lapse of tw minutes, TWO WHISTLES in rapid succes sion mean that the FUSE must be lighted : an after the lapse of five minutes more, THREE WHISTLES in rapid succession, and the lower ing of the RED FLAG, mean that all BLAST ING has ceased, and that the men can return to their working places.
3. When Blasting takes place during the Dinner hour, or immediately after working hours are over, the above signals (Flag and Whistles) must be strictly observed. Five minutes, however, must be allowed from the time the whistle to cease work has been blown before the first of the above signals are given
4. When the Whistle to cease work is blown before 5.30 p.m., no blasting can take place after 4 p.m.

## THE BARGAIN

The quarries ran on the 'bargain' system. The bargain was a piece of rock about six metres square, and members of the bargain team would be trained to work on the galleries – the high terraces in the rock where the slate was actually quarried – and in the sheds. A certain sum would be paid for good rock, a lower sum for rubble. The quarry steward's work then was to lower the price as far as he could by extolling the virtues of the rock; meanwhile the men would try to raise it by criticising the rock and pointing out its shortcomings. The wages of all members of the team depended on the results of this bargaining: no surprise, then, that this system was open to all sorts of manipulation.

In the meantime his partner would sit on a 'trafal', a straight edge of iron and steel set into a sloping piece of wood. He would trim the slate into a right angle with a guillotine knife, and then dress it to a particular size. This would all happen very quickly, almost without pause to draw breath, but although it might look effortless it called for a very keen eye and a sound understanding of the nature of the rock.

Later on electrically powered machines were used to saw and dress the slates. By using these in a damp atmosphere less damage was done to the quarrymen's lungs. But the machines could not do everything a human being could, and today slates are still split by hand in Wales.

Finally the slates would be weighed and carried on wagons down the incline [see p.15] and from there to Felinheli – or Port Dinorwic as it became known – to be exported, or to be stored for a while if the slate trade was not particularly flourishing.

## NAMES OF THE GALLERIES

All the galleries in the quarries had their own names. These often had a connection with historical events such as wars and battles (for example Crimea and Sebastopol in Penrhyn Quarry) or with local characters. Dinorwig quarrymen would sometimes boast that they had visited both Abyssinia and California on the same day! There were more homely names as well, such as Alice, Aberdaron and Princess May.

A number of the wagons in the Museum's collection still bear the names of the galleries where they were used.

## THE INDUSTRIAL REVOLUTION AND THE SLATE TRADE

People have been quarrying slate in north Wales for over 1,800 years. Slates were used to build parts of the Roman fort in Segontium in Caernarfon, and in Edward I's castle at Conwy.

But it was with the dawn of the Industrial Revolution in the 18th century that the slate industry really took off. As small villages such as Manchester exploded into large towns and then cities with the coming of mills and factories, there was an enormous demand for slates to roof the long terraces of houses built as homes for the workers – as well as the foundries and factories themselves.

In 1787 the 'Great New Quarry' of Dinorwig was opened by a partnership of three businessmen – one of them Thomas Assheton Smith – on the slopes between the present village of Dinorwig and Llyn Peris. By the 1870s Dinorwig Quarry employed over 3,000 men.

By then, slate quarrying was one of Wales's most important industries. Indeed, Wales produced over four-fifths of all British slates in this period, with Caernarfonshire the biggest producer among all Welsh counties. In 1882 the county's quarries produced over 280,000 tons of finished roofing slates, and in 1898 the slate trade in Wales as a whole reached its peak with 17,000 men producing 485,000 tons of slate.

## THE QUARRY

The quarry was a different world to the workshops. All the blasting work there meant that the mountain changed its shape and its geography on an almost daily basis. The galleries reared up to 650 metres above sea level. Yet the quarrymen knew every part of this maze of sheds and cabins and levels and paths by name.

# INJURIES, ILLNESS AND THE HOSPITAL

If there was an accident, quarrymen would go home. Stop work that day. Out of respect, you know.

The quarry was an extremely dangerous place. All the blasting work meant that unstable rock could fall without warning, burying workmen alive or sweeping them over precipices hundreds of metres high. Between 1822 and 1969, 362 men were killed altogether, although no more than three men were ever killed at one time. Most of these casualties were overwhelmed in rockfalls.

After a custom-built hospital was built on the shore of Padarn Lake in 1860, men who had had accidents would be taken there immediately to receive medical attention from the hospital doctor. There were a number of such doctors over the years. Perhaps the most famous of these was Dr Mills Roberts, an extremely able man by all accounts. He was also multi-talented: as well as playing football for Wales he was an excellent surgeon who could respond swiftly to the special

circumstances of the quarrymen's workplace. Dr Mills Roberts and the workshop smith once created two fully-functioning metal arms for a quarryman who had lost his own arms in an accident.

Long before the coming of the Welfare State, a shilling (5p) – the 'hospital shilling' – would be kept back from the men's pay so that the quarryman, or any member of his family who happened to fall ill, could be treated in hospital. It was also quite common to hold charity concerts, where members of the local community would perform for free to raise money for injured quarrymen and their families.

There were also more insidious threats to the quarrymen's health, especially tuberculosis and silicosis. Dr Mills Roberts gave the men and their families practical hints on healthy living: their houses should be well aired, they should wear flannel next to the skin and wash frequently. The quarryman should 'live for something beyond tea and bread-and-butter, and vary his diet with foodstuffs of all kind, particularly garden vegetables'. His injunction to 'Remember there is No Nourishment in Tea' is revealing, as for many years doctors had been blaming silicosis on the men's habit of drinking tea that was as strong as tar from being on the brew all day.

The Gilfach Ddu carpenters could apply their skills to any of the quarrymen's needs, including fashioning this wooden leg for an injured quarryman.

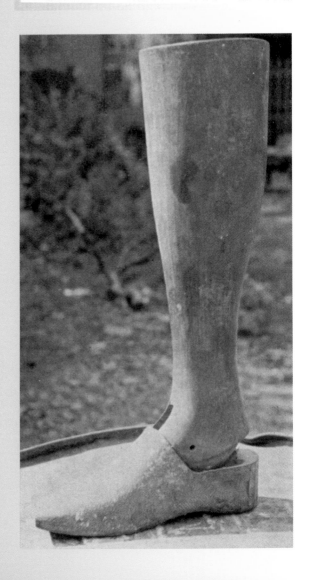

Penrhyn Quarry Hospital,
Bethesda, N. Wales.
6/1/22.

We have no case of Silicosis in this quarry of which I am aware, and I became convinced after four years' experience here that Slate dust is not merely harmless, but beneficial. The record of the men who have worked in the dusty shed at the mill since 1870 is available, and they were mostly alive prior to the war. I can send you a copy of the list. The light that recent research work has shared on the influence of dust inhalation upon the incidence of Phithisis all goes to support my view, and I would challenge anyone to prove otherwise.

J. BRADLEY HUGHES,
Medical Officer.

# THE INCLINE AND THE WAGONS – EXPORTING THE SLATE

The quarry owners invested heavily in building roads and railroads to improve the links between their quarries and the ports. As its English name, Port Dinorwic, suggests, the little fishing village of Felinheli (between Bangor and Caernarfon) was developed into an important port for exporting Dinorwig Quarry slate. In the beginning, the slates were carried in panniers on horseback to Cei Llydan, on boats to Cwm-y-Glo and then on wagons to Caernarfon and Felinheli. But it cost more to transport the slate than it did to produce it – in 1778, for example, it was more expensive to get the slates to Felinheli than it was to take them from there all the way to Liverpool!

In 1824 a horse tramway was built to connect the quarry and the port. But by 1848-9, an even more effective way of transporting the slates had been developed – the Padarn steam railway. Engines Jennie Lind and Fire Queen were regularly to be seen steaming back and forth to Penscoins, just above Felinheli. But how did they get the slates down the mountain to the trains?

This incline, named the V2, was restored to its original condition in 1998 thanks to a grant from the Heritage Lottery Fund and it is regularly to be seen working. In fact, this is the only such incline working in Britain today.

Getting the slates to the port was only the first step, of course. From there they went in their thousands on sailing ships and steamships to parts of Britain, northern Europe, North America and Australia

If you follow the signs to the incline you will see the answer: the slates were loaded onto wagons which travelled down the incline on rails to the bottom, where they were run off. Their weight would haul the empty wagons back up the incline on a parallel track, and the process began again.

## GILFACH DDU

The engineers of Gilfach Ddu prided themselves on the fact that they could build or mend almost any piece of equipment needed by the quarry or the port – everything from a chisel to a steam engine.

To do this they needed raw materials – wood and coal for example – and energy, supplied by the great water wheel [see p. 24].

There was always a lot of banter between the quarrymen and the workers of Gilfach Ddu.

As Gwilym Davies remembers:
*'They called us in the yard caterpillars because we ate but didn't produce anything.'*
And in Hugh Richard Jones's words:
*'They thought we didn't really do anything. That they kept us. That it wasn't the work that kept us, but the profit from their work. That's why the manager said that we were like caterpillars, eating all the profit.'*

But the daily labour at Gilfach Ddu was essential to the success of the quarry.

# THE ENGINEER'S HOUSE

This is the first building you will see when you turn left after the entrance. The Engineer was responsible for every aspect of the engineering work in the quarry, so it was convenient for him to live in a house that was part of the courtyard itself. Between 1870 and 1969, a series of engineers and caretakers and their families lived here for various periods. Today it is furnished as it would have been around 1911, with the red velvet curtains and the organ in the parlour reflecting a higher standard of living than the houses of the ordinary quarrymen in the village below. You can see a kitchen, parlour and living room of the period; the bedrooms upstairs have been turned into offices.

As the wash-house outside suggests, the women who lived in this house led physically demanding lives – what with washing, cleaning, baking, sewing and tidying, not to mention raising children. On top of all this, they had to keep the parlour immaculate in case of visitors, however much work, dust and noise went on in the yard itself.

This house, with its supply of electricity, would have been quite a bit more comfortable than the homes of the ordinary quarrymen and the men who worked in the yard – houses like the Fron Haul row [see p. 41], which you can explore beyond the café. But however comfortable the Engineer's house was, it was very humble indeed compared with Y Faenol, the magnificent manorhouse where the quarry owners lived. Today, however, it's an excellent place to show how ordinary people of this area lived and worked in the first decades of the 20th century.

*Learning more about the Chief Engineer's house in one of the Museum's events*

## THE BARRACKS

In contrast to the snug Engineer's House, the barracks were huts up on the hillside near the windswept galleries of the quarries where the men who travelled from afar to work in the quarry would stay during the week. In the past, men from villages on Anglesey, the other side of the Menai Straits, would leave home before three o'clock on Monday morning and walk to the

Moel y Don ferry. Once landed, they would walk from Port Dinorwic to Penscoins to catch the quarry train then climb up hundreds of metres to their barracks. And all this before doing a full day's work! Many of them would have smallholdings over on Anglesey and would bring their own food for the week – home-made bread and cheese and butter and bacon – in their 'wallets', long sacks of white linen. Reflecting the nature of this produce, the other quarrymen called these men *moch Môn* – 'Anglesey pigs'.

Each barrack had a living room and a bedroom, and space for four men. They were spartan enough – no electricity, very basic, rough furniture and a healthy population of fleas! The men would put brown paper in the window spaces to keep the wind out. And the wind could be piercing – one row of barracks near Aberdaron gallery was almost 650 metres above sea level and was christened 'Ireland View'.

## WHO OWNED THE QUARRY?

Local people had been working the mountain for centuries before Dinorwig Quarry opened. In 1788 Assheton Smith paid bailiffs to evict these people out of their tiny quarries.

By the end of the 19th century, almost all the land in Gwynedd was owned by just five families. The Assheton Smith family from Cheshire were the owners of Dinorwig Quarry. Their estate, Y Faenol on the banks of the Menai Straits, covered 34,000 acres of land. In George William Duff Assheton Smith's time, white cattle, deer and American bison, not to mention bears and monkeys, roamed Y Faenol's park. His brother Charles was more interested in the conventional gentlemanly amusements of the day – his race-horses won the Grand National four times, and he was besotted with racing yachts. Indeed, one of the quarry's steam engines, Pandora, was named after one of these boats.

Despite their upper-class pursuits and the yawning divide in living standards between the owners and the quarrymen, many of the Assheton Smith family were fair and conscientious masters. Although the relationship between themselves, their managers and the workers was a firmly hierarchical one, they could be kind; for example, they arranged for all the quarrymen to visit London in 1887 to enjoy Queen Victioria's Jubilee celebrations – a very rare opportunity for a holiday beyond Llanberis.

*Y Faenol, home of the Assheton Smith family, owners of the Dinorwig Quarry in the 19th century*

# TO STEAL A MOUNTAIN

The former Oil Store, beyond the Engineer's House, today houses an audio visual presentation. *To Steal a Mountain* tells the story of the quarry's development.

Pictures, words and music combine in a fascinating introduction to the quarryman's world. It's a story full of hope and magic as well as sadness and poverty.

There are regular showings of this presentation in French, German and Welsh as well as English.

# THE CABAN

The Caban was where Gilfach Ddu workers gathered in the lunch hour to eat their lunch and drink tea. This was their opportunity to socialise and to discuss current affairs; the Caban's President read aloud from the newspaper and announced details of local events such as concerts and special chapel services. It was an honour to be elected President of the Caban; it meant that the men greatly respected your wisdom and integrity. The men sat in a strict order based around the stove, which stood in the middle of the room radiating its welcome warmth; the youngest boys sat closest to the door. What with the stove and wet coats drying, the atmosphere in the Caban must have been warm but muggy – and the *ffowntan* (or 'fountain'), as the tea-urn was called, would be at a constant simmer, ready to brew the lunchtime tea. It was a cardinal sin to let it boil dry!

The quarrymen up on the galleries had their own cabanod, and often held eisteddfodau there, with all sorts of competitions from solo recitations to ambulance teams.

*You didn't need the 'Snowdon Echo' or any local paper. There were people from Waunfawr, Caernarfon, Llanrug, Cwm y Glo, all meeting there. So you knew what was happening in that village.*

*There was a huge red fire awaiting us all.*

## SOCIAL AND CULTURAL LIFE

At the height of the slate industry in Caernarfonshire, Llanberis and the surrounding district were a hive of activity of all kinds. For many, life outside working hours, especially in the years up to the Second World War, revolved to a great extent around the chapel; indeed the chapels closest to the quarry held special lunchtime chapel services so that the quarrymen could attend them in their lunch-hour. The chapel had its own rich cultural life, with prayer meetings and all kinds of societies. For those of a less devout disposition, there were plenty of chances to show off dramatic skills in myriad small clubs and societies, and the sounds of silver and brass bands practising for concerts and eisteddfodau rang around Llanberis and many of its surrounding villages. Sports were also popular, and there were plenty of football teams.

# THE SAWSHEDS

The three sawsheds at Gilfach Ddu held all kinds of specialist saws for different jobs of work, and like the carpenters' sheds are a clue to the great importance of wood in the workshops.

Firstly there was a large circular saw, used to cut lengthways through the great tree trunks brought here from Y Faenol estate. In the Vertical Saw Shed you can see a saw that actually consists of many parallel blades. This was used of course to saw the wood into planks, but it also produced the foundation timbers for the incline rails, beams for buildings, the mallets used by the quarrymen when splitting slate and legs for the tripod cranes that hoisted the slate blocks in the quarry.

The Sleeper Saw Shed contains two special saws; both were probably made in Gilfach Ddu. One was used to cut slots in the hardwood sleepers that supported the 61cm gauge tracks on the galleries, and the other was used to saw the wedges used to keep the railings tightly together.

*There was woodwork everywhere, we needed doors, windows, and lots of things ... there was plenty of work for carpenters*

# THE WATER WHEEL

Between 1870, when it was built by the De Winton company of Caernarfon, and 1925, when the smaller Pelton wheel came into use, this wheel supplied energy to all the Gilfach Ddu workshops. Today, its size still impresses: at 15.4 metres in diameter, it is the largest working water wheel in the UK.

The water powering the wheel comes from the Ceunant waterfall, above Llanberis, through cast iron pipes. The water then rises to the tank above the wheel (because the source is higher than the level of the tank). The wheel's propulsion comes from its rim rather than the axle and so the spokes of the wheel only serve to hold it together – rather like a bike wheel. By means of a system of cogs and pinion wheels, the energy from the water that flows from bucket to bucket on the wheel is transmitted along the line-shafting to all the workshops on site.

The wheel is so finely balanced that it begins to turn the minute just one of its 140 buckets fills with water. The wheel itself is a testament to the talent of local engineers, and still works perfectly a century and a half after it was built. Like the incline, the wheel was restored in 2000 thanks to a grant from the Heritage Lottery Fund, and it works continuously. Don't forget to climb the stairway or go up in the lift to see it close to – that way you will get a proper idea of the immense power of a wheel which powered all the workshops' activities.

Despite its efficient design, however, by 1925 the wheel had become badly worn through years of use. Every time the wheel broke down all work would come to a stop while it was mended. Instead a Pelton wheel was inserted on a branch of the main pipeline, in the corner under the larger wheel. Although it is so much smaller, this was more efficient than the large wheel as it was powered by kinetic energy (from water rushing through a pipe which gradually got narrower) rather than water falling from a great height, as in the case of the water wheel.

The Pelton wheel has only been known to fail once, during the hard winter of 1947, when the water froze in the pipes from the Ceunant waterfall.

## Key

1 Shop and entrance
2 Chief Engineer's House
3 Introductory film
4 Mess room
5 Temporary exhibition
6 Exhibition 'From Rock to Roof'
7 Slate splitting demonstrations
8 Sleeper Sawshed
9 Vertical Sawshed – way through to rear yard

10 Loco shed
11 Education and crafts room
12 Cafe and toilets
13 Fron Haul Quarrymen's Houses
14 Play area
15 Water wheel
16 Lift and stairs to water wheel
17 Entrance to the workshops

18 Power Hall
19 Foundry
20 Pattern Loft
21 Slate craft workshop
22 Blacksmith's Forge
23 Machine shop
24 Stores and clerk's office
25 Cropping shed
26 Painter's shed

This is an industrial museum. Please take care!

The door to the rear yard and the cafe and toilets will close half an hour before closing time.

toilets

wheelchair available for loan here

cafe

film

shop

hearing loop

water bowl for dogs

baby changing

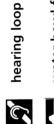

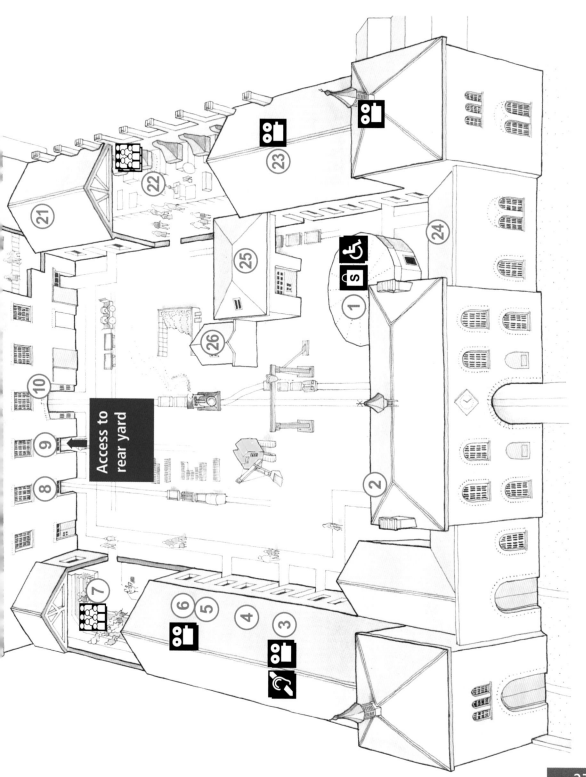

Access to rear yard

## ENERGY IN THE WORKPLACE

The energy created by the water wheel was carried to the various workshops by means of line shafting. The lines of this shafting system were effectively the workshops' arteries, the means by which lathes turned and hammers pounded, and saws and drills moved back and forth. They carried the power from the wheel to every part of the workshops, bringing life to machines that would otherwise lie still.

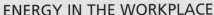

# THE FOUNDRY

This is where the workers produced the metal components for all sorts of machines and equipment used at Gilfach Ddu. It's a very good example of how self-sufficient these workshops were. This, too, is the highest room in the Museum – the height is necessary to house the 9.5 metre-high furnace, the crane and the jib.

The first step in producing the various components was carving the patterns for them. These were then placed on the foundry floor and packed round with special foundry sand. (You can see several patterns, in their moulding boxes, on the foundry floor.) After removing the pattern, the sand in the moulding boxes would be sufficiently compacted to receive the molten iron, which then hardened to the shape of the pattern.

Scrap iron, pig iron and cokes were transported to the foundry on small wagons. The layers of iron, alternating with layers of cokes, were fired in the furnace. When the iron was molten, the clay plug was pulled out of a hole at the bottom of the furnace. The molten iron would then flow along a chute and into the ladle.

From 1872 to 1966, when the foundry closed temporarily, the crane was used to raise and lower the moulding blocks. It was also used to hold a ladle steady to receive the molten iron from the furnace before moving it to its position above the mould, then pouring the iron. There is a smaller brass smelting furnace to the right of the cupola. This was used to cast bearings and other such pieces.

Working in the foundry on casting day could be hard, hot work and the men were allowed to go home early, as soon as they had finished casting. The foundry on a casting day was one of the warmest places in the workshops on a winter's morning!

# THE PATTERN LOFT

The pattern makers could produce a pattern for any metal object needed by the workshops: cogs, parts for steam engines – even the bell on the clock above the gateway to the workshops! The patterns were carved out of softwood. The pattern makers used some mechanical equipment – a pillar drill, fretsaw, lathe and whetstone – which, like the machines in all the other workshops, were driven by the line shafting. But they carved all the detailed, delicate carving work on the patterns by hand. Because of this, the other workers were not allowed in the Pattern Loft at all, in case they drew the

pattern maker's attention, causing his hand to slip and ruin the pattern. (However, it was whispered that there was a ghost in the pattern loft - so perhaps this spirit disrupted work from time to time!)

*Old William Jones was the pattern-maker there ... Although he did such detailed work on the patterns, what he had in those days was a piece of wood with four candles stuck to it. He used to have to move it around the table where he was working at the bench. It didn't throw a shadow on his work, you see. His work was that detailed.*

Unfortunately, the pattern loft mice were also very fond of the candles, so the quarry had to order specially unpleasant-tasting candles, just for use in the Pattern Loft.

Today you can see some of these fantastically intricate patterns – over 2,000 of them – in the pattern loft and in the new purpose-built storage facility that has been developed in order to preserve the patterns for the future. This means a rigorous process of numbering each item, photographing, weighing, measuring and then documenting each object so that it can be easily identified – which will provide valuable information in the future. Visitors can learn more about the process in the Pattern Loft's 'Behind the scenes' days, which run throughout the year.

## FATHER AND SON IN THE WORK-SHOPS/THE APPRENTICESHIP SYSTEM

*When you began, they gave you a hammer*

Most of the patterns in the Museum's collection were produced by members from the same Llanberis family, the Patrwm (Pattern) family as they were called. Eddie Patrwm was one of the last pattern makers to work in the yard, following in his father's and his grandfather's footsteps.

A boy who got work at the quarry was said to have 'found work'; he began as a rubbler, carting the waste rock away from the bargain. On the other hand, the boy who was apprenticed at Gilfach Ddu was said to have have 'found a place'. The standard of the apprenticeship in these workshops was recognised by employers and shipping companies all over the world. Gwilym Davies remembers his first day as an apprentice in the yard:

*New overalls and all. Overalls, and a cotton jacket, like denim you know, and my elder brother had bought me a saw in Gruffydd Jones, Caernarfon. A Henry Diston USA saw. And I can well remember the man in the shop saying, 'Open the box,' and there were three saws in it. Two going one way and one the other.*

*When I began as a young boy, you didn't get a wage in the yard. You worked for nothing for six months. You got sixpence for six months, the second half of the year ... during the second year you got nine pence a week in wages. And out of that you had to pay the hospital shilling every month.*

# THE LOCO SHED

This shed used to be called 'the Baltic' – presumably because it was so cold and draughty! Today the shed is home to Una, a 0-4-0, 61cm gauge steam engine, built in 1905 by Hunslet of Leeds. Una is

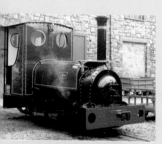

a good example of the kind of steam engines working in the quarries from the 1860s onwards. Without these engines, the quarries would not have developed as they did - railway connections could make or break a quarry. The shed is also home to Cilgwyn, a diesel locomotive, a Brush battery powered engine and a 1920's 'Royal Enfield' motorbike modified to run on the Quarry's narrow gauge rails.

You can also see three of the Museum's miniature locomotives here – Speedy, Dorothea and Countess. Una spent her working life at the Penyrorsedd quarry in the Nantlle Valley. She is steamed on a regular basis and is a splendid sight, steaming proudly along in her Midland Railway red livery.

A working steam engine is a romantic sight these days, in fact using the engine was anything but glamorous! The drivers and stokers were expected to arrive at the quarry by about 5 am to raise steam for the day's work, and also to sort out any small problems from the previous day. The stokers would couple and uncouple the wagons, on their knees in water, mud or snow, and attempt to get wagons back on the rails by brute force.

# LOCOMOTIVES, VELOCIPEDES AND CARRIAGES

Trains were used in the quarry to carry slates to port, and later to carry workers to their work as well. In 1848 two steam engines were running on the rails – *Jenny Lind* and the *Fire Queen*. In 1882 a strong, modern engine called Dinorwic was added to the stock. By 1895 two other large engines were travelling the line between Gilfach Ddu and Penscoins near Port Dinorwic – *Amalthaea* (called *Pandora* until 1909) and *Velinheli*.

These drew the workers' train until 1947, and the slate train too until 1961. The train only failed once in all this time, during the great snow of 1929.

Between 1848 and 1895, however, the workers used machines called 'velocipedes' to get to work.

These could move pretty quickly with a fair wind behind them! Indeed, although they were forbidden from doing so the men would often race their cars. In 1858 two men were drowned when they lost control of their car, tipping it into Padarn Lake.

Like everything else in the quarry, these had names – some fancy, like *Garibaldi*, *Signor Foli* and the *Duke of Cambridge*, and some more homely, such as *Y Gaseg* ('The Mare'), *Jennie Bach* ('Little Jennie') and *Y Falwoden Lwyd* ('The Grey Snail'). (You can see an example of a velocipede at the Museum.)

In 1895 over a thousand men were travelling back and forth every day between their homes and their work in the quarry and the workshops. Two carriages were added on Monday morning and Saturday afternoon to accommodate the workers from Anglesey, who only went home once a week.

This was the Assheton Smith family's private carriage, and as well as carrying the Faenol family and their guests on their occasional visits to the quarry, it carried the workers' wages every week from the bank in Port Dinorwic, guarded by two armed men.

There were all kinds of engines in the quarry; small ones used on the galleries to work drilling machines, and to draw sledges and rubble wagons, and larger engines which worked the slate run on the exit level railway. These were too large to work on the galleries.

There was also another kind of carriage on the line, a pretty remarkable one, called 'The Saloon' or *Y Garej Felen* ('The Yellow Carriage').

# SLATE SPLITTING AND DRESSING

At one time this workshop was a forge, and later it was a welding shop. It was in the quarry itself, in the *gwalia* – the open-sided sheds – that splitting and dressing was actually done; it is now carried out on the other side of the yard, but you can still see three slate sawing tables here. The power from the water wheel drives all three by means of the line shafting. The two smaller tables come from Dinorwig Quarry itself, but the largest comes originally from Penyrorsedd quarry in the Nantlle valley. It dates from 1876.

Slate sawing is a heavy, dusty and noisy task. A trough of water under the table cools the wheel as it cuts through the slab of slate, and damps down some of the dust produced. When a hundred or more tables were at work at the same time, there would be so much dust in the air that the further end of the shed would be invisible. The effects of this dust were very damaging to the quarrymen's health, leading to chest diseases and silicosis.

You will also see a number of slate dressing machines here: two guillotines worked by a drop lathe, to trim the slate, and three machines to dress the slate, one from Dorothea quarry, one from Penyrorsedd, and the third from Dinorwig. But remember that, although machine and electrical means have been devised to facilitate the work of sawing and dressing slates, they are still split by hand.

In their leisure hours, quarrymen were proud of their ability to work slate, fashioning it into beautiful, useful objects as well as roofing slates.

## WHAT DID QUARRYMEN WEAR?

Years ago the quarryman wore white clothes – white corduroy trousers, a fustian waistcoat and a white linen jerkin. He also wore a bowler hat and hobnailed boots. (Before safety helmets were devised, the hard bowler gave the head some measure of protection.) In bad weather he wore a coat of coarse tweed: on a rainy day, rather than a raincoat, he wore an old sack on his back. Most of the work clothes came from G.O. Griffith's shop in Caernarfon. As the famous Welsh novelist Kate Roberts, who was born in Rhosgadfan, Caernarfonshire in 1891, remembers, these clothes would have been physically difficult for the women to wash:

*The quarryman's wife dreaded washday... Mam, and I don't know how she did it, would carry this big, oval pan, with the working clothes in it, and put it under the water spout to rinse them, in all weathers.*

There are many examples in the quarrying areas of fireplaces, trays and panels delicately carved with all kinds of symbols, such as this example below.

## SLATE OF DIFFERENT SIZES

The slates were called by different names according to their sizes – and highly select names they were, too, varying from the 'Ladies' (16 inches by 12 inches) through 'Countesses' (20 inches by 12) and up through the 'Duchesses' and 'Princesses' to the 'Queens', which were 42 inches by 27.

It's difficult to know why men who spoke only Welsh gave the slates such very English names. It seems that the practice began at the end of the 18th century, at Penrhyn Quarry in Bethesda, introduced by a man called General Warburton.

## QUARRYING TERMS

*There was no English at all...everybody spoke Welsh.*

Although the quarry owners and stewards spoke English, the quarrymen and other workers spoke Welsh, a Welsh unique to their particular area. The very specialised craft of slate quarrying, and the close-knit nature of the community, meant that the quarry had a wealth of unique terms that gave the language of the quarrying areas its own very special, very colourful character. Here are some examples from Dinorwig Quarry:

*Bodiau llwyd:* literally, 'grey thumbprints', a fault in the slate in the form of a half circle like a thumbmark. This meant that the slate was too poor to be used for roofing slates.

*Cerrig hogia' bach:* literally, 'little boys' stones' – slates less than fourteen inches long. The rubbler would learn his craft by splitting and dressing these.

*A very special skill: slates are still dressed by hand today*

*Dros Bont Bala:* literally, 'over Bala bridge' – Bala bridge was the bridge by the quarry entrance. If a man 'went over' Bala bridge it meant he had been sacked.

*Ffarwel rock:* literally, 'Farewell rock' – rock so hard that the only thing to do was part company with it.

*Pen Bryn Sbïo:* literally, 'Lookout Hill' – a small hill about half way between the quarry and the powder house, where the explosives were kept. There was an excellent view of the village and the two lakes from here so it was the ideal spot to take a rest and have a smoke – taking care, of course, to keep the cigarettes far enough away from the powder bag!

# THE FORGE

*There were great lads there, lots of stories...and that big old hammer pounding away.*

Although every workshop had its own, important part to play in the work of Gilfach Ddu, in many senses the forge was at the heart of the work. Various components produced in other parts of the yard came together here in the form of sprockets or chains, axles and wheels. At one time twelve fires burned in twelve hearths as a team of smiths struck and forged the metal pieces produced by the other workshops into equipment of all kinds.

These were industrial blacksmiths, then, not farriers. The quarryman's tools were essential to him in his work, and a good blacksmith understood the differing needs of various quarrymen. This meant that he could make tools that met the needs of different men and different kinds of rock. One of the first tasks for an apprentice blacksmith would be to forge his own tongs, pincers and swages.

The great double doors between the forge and the cropping shed were a convenient way to get large items into the forge, and an easy way too to get at the cokes that fed the fires. In the yard's heyday the heat of the flames must have been sweltering, and the clamour of the hammers as they struck the anvils almost deafening.

Like the forging hammer, which dates from 1900, the pneumatic hammer of 1924-5 that can be seen here is powered by energy from the water wheel. So too is the big grindstone that stands at one end of the workshops. The wooden benches and vices used by the smiths to hold the equipment still stand against the walls of the forge.

Now there are four hearths here, and one smith, who still does much repair work on the Museum's equipment. He also makes beautiful objects of steel, like the daffodil seen here, which is on sale in the Museum shop.

# THE YARD AND THE CROPPING SHED

There are a variety of different machines to be seen in the yard. These include two cranes, one which used to unload slates at Port Dinorwic, with a steam engine, the second, a diesel excavator from the 1930s, showing the new generation of diesel machinery.

*Wagons everywhere – wagons waiting to be mended, wagons already mended and painted red with big numbers on them ... spare wheels everywhere.*

The Cropping Shed contains some of the largest machines in the workshops, including the cutter or shears itself, with its powerful blades, used to cut through thick steel. Here too you can see one of Dinorwig Quarry's old receivers (although nowadays a modern electrical engine blows air into it): this is the air that rushes through the horn on the external wall from time to time during the day. This is the 'Fire Engine' hooter, one of two at the quarry. The *caniad* ('call') first thing in the morning and then at regular times during the day, denoting blasting times in the quarry, was a familiar sound to the people of Llanberis and the surrounding area.

The compressor also blew compacted air through a network of pipes that extended all over the quarry. These pipes supplied compressed air to drive the drilling machines used at the rockface.

You can also see lifting gear, or the 'blondin', as it was called by the quarrymen, after the famous tightrope walker of the 19th century. This equipment was used to raise loaded wagons from the bottom of deep holes or 'sinks'. This example comes from Penyrorsedd quarry in the Nantlle valley, and is remarkable because it shows the use of electricity in a quarry in the period before 1914. The blondin driver's task demanded fierce concentration, as one slip could mean death at the bottom of the 'sink'. The electricity came from the Cwm Dyli Power Station in Nant Gwynant, still at work today.

# THE REPAIR WORKSHOP AND THE MACHINE WORKSHOPS

These workshops are testimony to the self-sufficiency of Gilfach Ddu: the variety and size of the machinery on display also gives some idea of the technical abilities of the staff employed here. In the repair workshops you can see many unique items from the Museum's collection. Among them there is a riveted boiler for a narrow gauge engine. This boiler was built in the company's boiler workshops at Port Dinorwic, and it gives you some idea of the high standard of craftsmanship needed to make a boiler out of riveted plates – one which could withstand a pressure of over 25kg to the square centimetre. On one of the other benches you will see a number of cans and tins, including the small round tins used to pay the quarrymen. These were made by the quarry's tinsmith, and were mainly used to store paraffin or oil of different sorts. Here too you can see a pump used to drive water up to the quarry hospital, some 500 metres away.

In the machine shop there is a lathe dating from 1900, used for turning all sorts of things – from the incline drum's wheels to turntables. There is also another lathe, 6.4 metres long, used to turn the transmission and propeller shafts for the company's fleet of steam ships. The slotting machine, on the other hand, was used to cut keyways in gear and pinion wheels, sprockets and drive pulleys. There is also a rope-weighing scale. The quarrymen themselves paid for their ropes and were responsible for caring for them (as well as their explosives, their chisels and other tools). So it paid them to take great care of ropes that would be bearing their whole weight – sometimes on a rock face hundreds of metres high.

Most of the machines to be seen in these workshops could still do a good day's work, and indeed some of them are still used from time to time.

# WAGES AND PAYING THE MEN

Although the Gilfach Ddu workers were skilled and able craftsmen, they had no paper qualifications, and were paid as ordinary workers. For example, the salary of a fitter, carpenter or smith in 1917 was 4/2 [21p] a day. If he happened to be a particularly able craftsman, who had been perfecting his craft for years, he might get 4/6 a day. A foreman – who was not only a craftsman of the highest calibre but also shouldered much responsibility – was paid no more than 5 shillings [25p] a day in the same period.

The quarrymen and the men of Gilfach Ddu worked all year round, apart from Saturday afternoons and Sunday. They had few holidays. According to Alwyn Owen, *When I began, you only got Christmas Day ... and the Saturday, Good Friday and Easter Monday. Then they gave you Labour Day in May and Harvest Monday. Those were the holidays.* Hugh Richard Jones adds, *In winter we wouldn't see daylight until Saturday. It was dark – you'd work from six in the morning till six at night.*

At the beginning the quarrymen were paid every four weeks, on Saturday - called *Sadwrn setlo* ('settling-up Saturday') or *Diwrnod Cyfri Mawr* ('Day of the Great Pay Count'). In time this became fortnightly pay and then a weekly paypacket. The wages came in little round tins that were placed in neat rows on a large tray. The head clerk would then call the number of the tin and the right man would step forward to claim his money.

If it had been a particularly good month, the tin would be too small to hold all the money. This happened very seldom but when it did, the rest of the money would be put in an envelope and given to the man along with his tin - so a month like this was called *mis enfilop* - an 'envelope month'.

*We'd go up - there were steps going up... from Gilfach Ddu to the Main Office ... by the end they were calling them the Golden Steps. We used to walk up there to get our wages ...*

*In those days the wages in the yard were low, you know ... all the craftsmen, carpenters and smiths and fitters. They all got the same wages.*

# STORES, CLERK'S OFFICE

These rooms housed the quarry administration. This is where the telephone equipment connecting various parts of the quarry to the workshops was kept. This, too, is where the stores were kept. In the main stores, iron, steel and other large items were kept on long racks. There was also an amazing variety of screws, nails and washers, with every drawer correctly and minutely labelled. Once, a tally board hung by the door in this place (you can see it now through the entrance archway window). Every man who worked in Gilfach Ddu had his own tally, to be presented at the end of the day. Men who called at the stores were not allowed to go into the stores themselves – they had to ask for what they needed at an adjacent window. A notice warned that they should not linger too long!

# 1-4 FRON HAUL

In 1998 work began on an exciting and ambitious project: moving a row of four houses from Fron Haul in Tanygrisiau near Blaenau Ffestiniog to the National Slate Museum. This row had been condemned by Gwynedd County Council because of its poor condition. The houses themselves are typical of the cramped terrace housing to be seen all over the quarrying areas. The Museum realised that this offered the perfect opportunity to bring the history of these areas to life again, and decided that the houses should reflect three historical periods and three areas of paramount importance to the history of the slate industry.

## No 3
## (Tanygrisiau near Blaenau Ffestiniog, 1861)

At this period the slate industry was rapidly becoming one of the most important industries in Wales, and the main employer in Gwynedd. As demand for slates grew, workers moved from the surrounding rural parishes to work in an industry that was demanding, dirty and dangerous, but paid a better wage than labouring on local farms. Between 1831 and 1881 the population of Ffestiniog parish grew from 1,648 to 11,274. Housing could not keep up with this and two families would often share one house, or a friend or relation would lodge with them. In 1861 the inhabitants of this house were a married couple: William Williams, a quarryman who hailed from Trawsfynydd in Meirionethshire and Elen Williams, from Llanbedr also in Meirionethshire. William's brother and a lodger from Anglesey lived there too. Any children in a family would share a room with their parents, sometimes sharing the same bed, or sleep in a makeshift bed on the floor. Dampness, the water supply and sewerage were also a problem, and typhoid and tuberculosis were constant threats because of this.

*The Fron Haul houses in their original site*
*(illustration by Falcon Hildred)*

*No. 2 Fron Haul, Bethesda 1901*

*No. 1 Fron Haul, Llanberis, 1969*

## No. 2:
## The Penrhyn Strike
## (Bethesda, 1901)

Penrhyn Quarry, the other side of the mountain to Dinorwig, was the only rival in size, productivity and importance throughout most of the nineteenth century. In November 1900 2,800 quarry-men walked out of the quarry. This was the beginning of an exceptionally bitter and long-running dispute – one of the worst in British industrial history. The strike itself lasted through three years of grinding poverty and despair, but in June 1901 500 men went back to work at the quarry and from then on there were very strong feelings in the Bethesda area about the *Bradwyr* or 'Traitors'.

*No. 3 Fron Haul, Tanygrisiau, 1861 (see p. 41)*

## No. 1:
## Dinorwig Closes
## (Llanberis, 1969)

You can see at once how different this house looks to the others, with its rendered yellow frontage and blue paintwork. This is Llanberis in 1969. In July of this year, Prince Charles was invested Prince of Wales in Caernarfon Castle, on a dais of Dinorwig slate. In August, Dinorwig Quarry closed: 350 men lost their work during their annual holiday. Little did they know, as they left the quarry and workshops at the beginning of the holidays, that they would never return. This house, as in the previous house, presents a typical family. The husband has just been told that he is out of a job, in an area where unemployment already runs high. He may get a job in one of the few factories in the Caernarfon area or

within the tourist industry. The mother works in a local clothes factory, 'the women's quarry' – and the home is no longer women's only domain. Their son is at school, a focus for new themes and issues – for example the strong feelings of some of the local people against the Investiture. The fashion of the day is plainly seen in this house in the kitchen units, lighting equipment, the colourful carpets and curtains, the single records and the clothes.

No. 4 is used as an education house for group visits: a good place to hear a story, draw a picture, or find out more about the people who lived in Fron Haul.

*'It's not a house that makes a home – not walls and doors and windows and hearth – but the things in the house, the cloth on the table, the flower pot with its fern in the window ... the coat hanging behind the door.' (T. Rowland Hughes, from his novel **O Law i Law** ['From Hand to Hand'])*

## HOW DID WE MOVE FRON HAUL?

The houses were moved by the team from St Fagans: National History Museum, near Cardiff, which has over fifty years' experience of moving and re-erecting historic buildings, including a row of ironworkers' houses from Rhyd-y-car near Merthyr

Tydfil. During 1998 all the bricks and stones of Fron Haul were individually numbered,

like a giant jigsaw, and carefully transported to Llanberis. The first record of the houses is in the Census of 1861: thanks to a grant from the National Lottery Heritage Fund the row was formally opened in its new home in July 1999.

## LIVING CONDITIONS AND A WOMAN'S PLACE

Although many women went out to work before they were married – usually into service, as maids – after marriage very few women worked outside the home. Most agreed that the woman's place was in the home, caring for the children and making sure there was food on the table and peace on the hearth when her husband came home from work. Most of the quarryman's wages went straight to his wife for household expenses. Living on low wages called for thrift and careful planning, and the family's food was very plain. As Alwyn Owen remembers about the money, 'We saw it, we took it home – and that was it.'
The furniture, decoration and general standard of living in the quarrymen's houses were very similar to each other. There was little money left over to buy ornaments or extra trimmings

*Make sure you have a cupboardful of food, a coalhouse full of coal, a clean house and no grandness. You can't eat grandness.*
[A quarryman father's advice to his daughter on her wedding day.]

Although many of the families in the villages around Llanberis kept smallholdings and fattened a pig or a calf, the whole area depended for its livelihood on the slate industry. Gwilym Davies remembers, 'There was nothing but the quarry. No factory or anything. The quarry: or the parish.' The quarryman's life was hard and physically demanding, and the wife's domestic skills enabled her husband to work longer hours and earn a little more money. Her life was also physically demanding, at a time when a family of six or seven children was the norm, and there were no appliances like washing machines and vacuum cleaners. A quarryman's house was his home: for his wife, it was also her workplace.

## THE QUARRY CLOSES, THE SLATE INDUSTRY TODAY

*There wasn't a last day.*

*It had slackened an awful lot. But nobody thought it would close down that suddenly.*

The Penrhyn Strike of the early 1900s greatly affected the whole of the north Wales slate market. Compared with the situation before the Strike, for three whole years this huge quarry supplied the world with very few slates. Many companies who had been keen buyers of Welsh slates turned to other suppliers during this time and never returned.

The Second World War further affected the slate industry as the demand for building slates fell considerably, and many of the quarrymen enlisted in the army.

Although there was a spurt of post-war building activity, the north Wales slate industry never really returned to the level of productivity it had enjoyed at the turn of the century. During the 1950s it became obvious that the quarry was more or less worked out, and although there were attempts to find good rock and to diversify, Dinorwig Quarry closed without warning in August 1969.

The quarry's equipment and fittings were put up for auction and many of the items you can see in the Museum today were only saved from the auctioneer's hammer by the sterling efforts of a few former workers. According to Hugh Richard Jones:

*They'd already sold some things, and what frightened me most was to see them up on the big [water] wheel...they were going to burn it as scrap. I got the chance to stop them doing that, and talked to the receiver and the auctioneer, and they closed the whole lot up and got the 'vultures' out of there. That's what we called them, those scrap merchants – 'vultures' because they would take the whole lot. Whatever they saw, they'd take it, store it then burn it.*

The Museum was opened to the public in 1972 with Hugh Richard Jones, former chief engineer, as manager.

Many of Dinorwig's former quarrymen and engineers were employed to present and interpret their craft, and a collection of significant examples of equipment was begun, often collected from other Welsh slate quarries. This is still the policy today: we're proud of the opportunity to use knowledgeable staff, who understand the amazing history of the slate industry.

And that industry still exists. About 200 people are currently employed in Wales's slate quarries, with a large number working for Welsh Slate in Penrhyn Quarry, Bethesda and in smaller quarries belonging to the same company around Blaenau Ffestiniog and the Nantlle Valley. The historic J.W. Greaves company still works in Llechwedd Quarry, Blaenau Ffestiniog; and the Wincilate company still works at Aberllefenni, though not now from the underground slate mine nearby, which has closed. Further south, a slate quarry has reopened near the village of Cilgerran, producing blocks for walling. The foundation of the industry is still producing roofing slates, but Welsh slate is also used for architectural purposes, for example the Cwt-y-Bugail slate in the Museum's shop and cafe, and for many other uses, for instance foundations for roads.

# INFORMATION FOR VISITORS

### THE SHOP
The striking, octagon-shaped shop built of local slate is the entrance to the Museum. There's also an excellent choice of gifts and items to take home with you. The shop sells fine foods from Wales such as biscuits and jam; guide-books and maps to help you enjoy the glorious countryside around you; elegant jewellery – some made from silver and slate, and perfect for gifts; and unique craft items produced at Gilfach Ddu itself.

### TOILETS
Men's, women's and disabled toilets are situated in the Ffowntan. There are also baby-changing facilities in the women's and disabled toilets.

### THE FFOWNTAN
The Museum's cafe, the Ffowntan, is named after the urn in the Caban which boiled water for the men's tea. It serves a variety of delicious home-made food, from hot meals to light snacks such as soup or salad.

Try one of the excellent cakes or an ice cream, or if you'd like a glass of beer or wine with your food the restaurant is licensed. There are a number of picnic tables outside the café for those who prefer to eat outside.

# Information

## ACCESS FOR LESS ABLED VISITORS

### Wheelchair users
It is possible to take wheelchairs to every part of the site (including the Ffowntan and the toilets), except for the pattern loft and into the Fron Haul houses. (However, it is possible to get up the path as far as the front doorway of each house.) There is a lift to the water wheel and the path to the incline is accessible to wheelchair users. There are designated disabled parking bays in the parking area. A wheelchair is available on request in the shop.

### For visitors with visual and hearing impairments
One of the great joys of visiting a museum like the National Slate Museum is the experience of the noises and smells of the exhibits and demonstrations. Few objects are in glass cases, and the Museum Assistants and craftsmen are happy to allow visitors to touch and handle exhibits and demonstrations, and to explain their role – just ask! Video presentations can be seen throughout the Museum, and headsets can be worn in To Steal a Mountain. Guide dogs are welcome and water bowls are provided at the entrance, near the quarrymen's houses and outside the Ffowntan.

### Play area
This is a great place for children to play safely and learn at the same time. Suitable for children under 12, children must be supervised at all times.

### Events
A number of very popular seasonal events are held at the Museum at different times of year. These include Halloween, the Winter Fair and St David's Day. Special activities for children at the Museum make the summer and half-term holidays extra fun.

### Parking
There is ample parking space in front of the Museum. A daily charge is made for cars but there is no charge for coaches. The car park is operated by Gwynedd County Council.

### Group visits
If you are interested in arranging a group visit please phone beforehand to discuss your requirements.

*'One of the best Museums we have ever visited'*

*'The atmosphere is great'*

*'Friendly staff, full of information'*

*'Very special – and the food is lovely'*
*'Inspiring'*

## Location

The National Slate Museum
Gilfach Ddu
Parc Padarn
Llanberis
Gwynedd
LL55 4TY
Tel: (01286) 870630 Fax: (01286) 871906
Email: slate@museumwales.ac.uk
www.museumwales.ac.uk

The National Slate Museum is situated nine miles from Caernarfon, twelve miles from Bangor and seventeen miles from Betws y Coed. Follow the signs from junction 11 of the A55. There is a regular bus service from Caernarfon and Bangor to Llanberis and Sherpa bus services into Snowdonia start from Llanberis. Please phone the Museum for more details.

## Padarn Country Park

Padarn Country Park is an eight hundred acre site embracing two Sites of Special Scientific Interest and a Local Nature Reserve. You can walk for miles along the banks of beautiful Padarn Lake on specially constructed walkways, or follow a nature trail or an industrial archaeology path around Vivian Quarry. As well as the Museum itself, the Park's attractions include the Padarn Lake Railway, where you can travel on a steam train along the lake shore and the ropes and ladders centre, next to the Museum.

## Some other books to read

There are a number of general guides to the slate industry, of which the best are probably:

*The North Wales Quarrymen 1874-1922* by R. Merfyn Jones (University of Wales Press)

*A Gazeteer of the Welsh Slate Industry* (Gwasg Carreg Gwalch, out of print)

*The Slate Industry* (Shire Publications)

The Museum shop also has various specialised guides to specific aspects of the industry, such as transport and machinery.

The slate quarrying areas of north Wales have bred many fine novelists, some of whose work is available in translation. Kate Roberts' *Feet in Chains* ('*Traed mewn Cyffion*', John Jones Publishing, out of print) is a powerful portrait of life in these areas in the 1890s. *One Moonlit Night* ('*Un Nos Ola' Leuad*', Canongate Books) by Caradog Prichard, who was a journalist in Fleet Street for many years, is a colourful, affecting, sometimes disturbing account of his childhood in Bethesda in the early years of the twentieth century.

As well as some of the books mentioned above the Museum shop also sells guidebooks, Ordnance Survey Maps and books of general interest.

## Acknowledgements

The oral testimony qoted in this book comes from interviews with Alwyn Owen, Gwilym Davies and Hugh R. Jones, all ex-quarrymen. The full interviews are in the sound archive at St Fagans: National History Museum.

Photograph of slates on page 8 © Alfred McAlpine Slate.

Photograph on page 20 © Wales Tourist Board.

Black and white photographs on pages 2,4,10,11,12,13,15,17,21,22,28,32,33,34 © Gwynedd Archives and Museums Services.

Thanks to all the above for permission to use their images.

# TIMELINE: SOME IMPORTANT DATES

500 million years ago: The creation of slate

1300s   Cilgwyn Quarry, Nantlle, is in production

**1700s**
1787   Dinorwig Quarry is established
1790   Port Penrhyn is developed for export business

**1800s**
1801   Penrhyn Tramway opens
1818   Welsh Slate Company's quarry opens in Blaenau Ffestiniog
1820   Construction of Porthmadog harbour
1830   Penybryn Quarry, Nantlle, is the first user of chain inclines
1848   Steam locomotives are first used on the Padarn Railway
1874   North Wales Quarrymen's Union is established
1874   Steam locomotives are introduced at Port Penrhyn
1881   Ffestiniog parish has over 11,000 inhabitants
1890   Hydro-electricity is first used at Llechwedd Quarry

**1900s**
1900-3   The Penrhyn strike, one of the longest in British labour history
1918   Minimum wage is agreed by quarry owners and union officials
**1920s**   Crushing mills are erected at Penrhyn Quarry, to grind slate waste used in road construction
**1940s**   Slate waste is used to make building blocks
1964   The Alfred McAlpine company purchases Penrhyn Quarry
1969   Closure of Dinorwig Quarry
1972   National Slate Museum opens
1999   A large shipment of slates from Penrhyn Quarry is sent to Australia, to use for storm repairs
2007   The Lagan family, from Belfast, become owners of the Penrhyn Slate Quarry